Mrs. William H. Nash

Cloud City Cook-Book

Mrs. William H. Nash

Cloud City Cook-Book

ISBN/EAN: 9783744781275

Printed in Europe, USA, Canada, Australia, Japan

Cover: Foto ©Lupo / pixelio.de

More available books at **www.hansebooks.com**

"CLOUD CITY"

Cook Book.

CLOUD CITY

COOK·BOOK.

LEADVILLE, COLORADO.
Herald Democrat Steam Book and Job Printing House.
1889.

PREFACE.

"Of making many books there is no end," said a wise man; but probably he had good cooks. There is a "place" for all things as well as a "time," and every hungry man knows the place for a good dinner. If the shortest road to man's heart is by way of his stomach, then the projectors of this little volume think they have struck it rich. So, like all other authors, we have written to meet a "long felt want." There are cook-books and cook-books, but who ever saw a cook-book for "Cloud City"? It is a well-established fact that in a high altitude the science culinary has its local and peculiar laws. It is commonly held that a different proportion of ingredients is necessary, as well as a different length of time. It is even claimed by some that more fuel is required here than in a lower altitude. Be this as it may, it is well established that the husband, who has recently brought his wife from the East, is not in healthy employment when he reminds her of the superior quality of his mother's cooking. He must wait until she has learned the new conditions in her new world. Without a scientific explanation of why the boiling point is reached at lower temperature here than at lower altitude, or whether this one fact accounts for the necessity of different proportions of ingredients in cookery, the Ladies of the Congregational Church gracefully bow themselves before the public with a genuine blessing to every family. Poor cooking is responsible for much of the wretched health of women and children, and much of the drinking habit among men. If, by gathering together in this little volume the wisest experience, wrought out in the peculiar conditions of this lofty altitude, we are able to bring peace and happiness to the home, our ambition shall have been amply satisfied.

LADIES CONGREGATIONAL CHURCH.

Soups.

PEA SOUP.

Parboil the peas in saleratus water (one heaping teaspoon to kettle two-thirds full of water), then wash well and put in to boil with a piece of salt pork. Season to taste, with salt and pepper, and onions previously fried in butter. Add dried bread crumbs just before serving.—MRS. C. H. BAILEY.

TOMATO SOUP.

One quart of tomatoes, or a two-pound can of tomatoes, to which add one quart water, one-half of a small onion sliced, a piece of butter the size of a hen's egg, in which rub a large table-spoon of flour, and boil slowly one hour. Just before serving, strain the soup and add one pint of scalded milk.

BLACK BEAN SOUP.

One pint of black beans, a small joint or shank of beef, a slice of salt pork. Soak the beans over night, drain off the water, and put them into the kettle with the meat, and cover with water. Boil about five hours; strain through the colander. Season with red pepper and a little wine. Add the yolks of three hard-boiled eggs and slices of lemon.—MRS. WERNER.

VEGETABLE SOUP.

Boil a soup-bone all day in plenty of water; strain it, add a little salt, and let it stand until the next day. In the morning, boil steadily until about an hour before dinner, when season to taste, and add one large onion, part of a carrot, little cabbage, one tomato, part of a turnip, one potato, all chopped very fine.—Mrs. Hugh Parry.

ONION SOUP.

Four large onions, cut up (not sliced), six ounces of butter, salt, cayenne, soup stock, with yolks of four eggs, one-fourth of a loaf of bread cut in very thin slices and dried, two tablespoons of grated cheese. Slowly stir the onions in the butter one hour, stirring frequently, being very careful not to brown; add salt, pepper, cayenne and stock, and cook one hour longer. Add one-third as much stock. Have in the tureen the bread and cheese. Beat up the eggs with a ladle full of soup; pour this on the bread, cover close, and stand five minutes. Add the rest of the soup and serve at once.—Mrs. Werner.

MACARONI SOUP.

One gallon soup stock, five sticks macaroni, one onion. Season with salt and pepper. Boil well.—Mrs. Hugh Parry.

VEAL SOUP.

Two legs of veal, put on with boiling water and skimmed; when skimmed, add butter. Prepare rice by boiling. When the soup is done, remove bone and meat, strain, add rice, and let come to a boil. Beat yolk of egg in dish with a little water, add chopped parsley, little nutmeg; then pour over soup and serve.

RICE SOUP.

One quart of water, one-fourth cup of rice, piece of butter, yolk of egg, chopped parsley, little nutmeg. Stir the yolk of the egg, add parsley and nutmeg; pour over the soup and serve.

NOODLE SOUP.

Boil two good, fat old chickens until all that is good of them is extracted for the broth. For the noodles, take two eggs, a pinch of salt, three tablespoons sweet milk, flour enough to make a stiff dough. Roll out in two *very thin* sheets; let dry until they will roll without breaking. Lay the sheets together, roll up tight, and cut as fine as possible with a sharp knife into little ribbons. Throw the noodles into the boiling broth about twenty minutes before serving.—MRS. WERNER

ASPARAGUS OR CELERY SOUP.

Six bunches of asparagus, cooked thoroughly and pressed through a sieve; one quart of milk, half pound butter, and four tablespoons flour. Mix flour and butter together, and let boil five minutes, then add the milk, then the asparagus stirring well but not boiling. Season with salt and pepper to taste. If not perfectly white, strain again, and serve hot. If celery is used, three bunches are sufficient; the soup to be made same as above.—MRS. HUGH PARRY.

YEAST.

Peal and boil eight common-sized potatoes in two quarts of water, with one handful of hops tied up in a thin bag. When the potatoes are done, mash them fine, add one pint of flour, one tablespoon ginger, and one-half cup sugar; mix thoroughly, then, having added more water to make up for what has boiled away, turn on the water in which the potatoes and hops were boiled, boiling hot, stirring it well. When quite warm, but not hot, add one cup of yeast. After it is done working, add one tablespoon salt.—MRS. C. H. BAILEY.

GRAHAM BREAD.

Two cups graham flour, one and a half cups sour milk, one tablespoon N. O. molasses, one scant tablespoon soda, one tablespoon salt.—MISS F. L. RAYMOND.

BISCUIT.

One quart flour, one cup lard, two teaspoons Price's baking powder, sifted with flour. Salt. Mix with milk to roll soft, and bake in a quick oven.—MRS. BROOKS.

YEAST.

Boil six potatoes until soft, mash them through a colander, add enough of the water they were boiled in to make a thin batter; then six tablespoons sugar. Stir all together with a large cup full of fresh yeast, and put in a warm place over night.

S. N. DWIGHT, President.   M. H. WILLIAMS, Vice-President.
J. N. WALLING, Cashier.   T. H. LEE, Ass't Cashier.

The American National Bank

LEADVILLE, COLO.

Capital, - - $100,000.

DIRECTORS:

M. H. WILLIAMS,   T. G. ROBERTS,   H. S. DICKERMAN,

S. T. KOSTITCH,   DANIEL SAYER,

GEORGE P. COPELAND,   CHAS. A. SEYMOUR,   SAM. MAYER,

GEORGE E. TAYLOR,   J. N. WALLING,

S. N. DWIGHT.

A general banking business transacted. Deposits received payable on demand. Time loans made on satisfactory security and commercial paper discounted. Drafts issued on principal cities of United States and Europe. Careful attention given to collections. All customers treated in the most liberal manner consistent with sound banking.

FAIRBANK'S ✦ SOAPS.

WHITE STAR,	100	Bars,	-	75 Pounds.
"	50	"	-	37 "
"	25	"	-	$18\frac{3}{4}$ "
MASCOT,	100	"	-	75 "
CLAIRETTE,	100	"	-	75 "
FAIRY, Large,	100	"	-	66 "
" Small,	100	"	-	$37\frac{1}{2}$ "
GOLD DUST POWDER,	24	Pack'gs,	72	"

The above Soaps are skillfully manufactured from the very best material, and are not excelled in quality by any in the world.

Yours truly,

N. K. FAIRBANK & CO.,

Factories: St. Louis and Chicago.

The above goods are carried in stock and can be obtained from

YOUR GROCER.

HOP YEAST.

Boil four large potatoes, and at the same time steep a fourth package of hops in sufficient water to cover them. Mash the potatoes through a colander, strain over them four cups of the hop water; add one cup sugar, tablespoon salt; thicken with flour to the consistency of batter cakes. Add one-half cup yeast, and leave it uncovered in a jar to rise. Use one-half a cup of this for four loaves of bread.—Mrs. WERNER.

GRAHAM GEMS.

One pint graham flour, one pint flour, one-half cup sugar, one pint sour milk, little salt, and small teaspoon soda.—Mrs. W. H. NASH.

MUFFINS.

One cup sweet milk, two eggs well beaten, one small teaspoon salt, two large teaspoons baking powder, flour for stiff batter. Drop in hot muffin pans.—Mrs. J. M. RAYMOND.

GRAHAM GEMS.

One cup sour milk, tablespoon of molasses, pinch of salt, half teaspoon soda, graham flour.—Mrs. HUGH PARRY.

BOSTON BROWN BREAD.

Two cups sour milk, one cup sweet milk, one-half cup molasses, two cups Indian meal, two cups graham flour, one teaspoon salt, one teaspoon soda. Steam five hours. Bake one-half hour in a slow oven.—Mrs. J. M. RAYMOND.

BROWN BREAD.

Four cups milk, three cups Indian meal, one cup graham flour, one cup flour, one cup molasses, one egg, teaspoon soda dissolved in a little boiling water, one teaspoon salt. Steam five or six hours. Bake half an hour. (This rule requires a five-pound lard pail to steam).—Mrs. W. H. NASH.

GRAHAM GEMS.

Two cups graham meal, two cups flour, three cups sour milk, two large spoons sugar.   Salt.   Soda according to condition of the milk.—Mrs. C. H. Bailey.

GRIDDLE CAKES.

One cup sour milk, one cup sweet milk, two eggs, half teaspoon soda, one small teaspoon baking powder.   Mix with flour. —Mrs. Guilrault.

POTATO BREAD.

Six good-sized potatoes, boiled and well mashed; one pint or more of the water in which they were boiled, one cup of yeast for the sponge.   Set the sponge in a warm place over night.   In the morning, when kneading the bread add a little salt, little sugar, lard the size of an egg, and sufficient luke-warm water to make six loaves of bread.—Mrs. Hugh Parry.

GRIDDLE CAKES.

One cup stale bread crumbs soaked in two cups of water, three cups flour, one yeast cake to start.   Let it rise over night; in the morning add two eggs and one-half teaspoon soda, and milk to form a thin batter.   The batter left can be used successive mornings, the same as buckwheats.

RUSK.

One pint milk and one pint sugar; warm slightly, add one-half cup yeast, raisins and some flour.   Let set over night, and in the morning add salt, three beaten eggs, one heaping cup melted butter and more flour.   Let it rise, then make into rolls and when light bake.—Mrs. O. H. Simons.

BISCUIT.

One cup sweet milk, two teaspoons baking powder sifted in flour, one small teaspoon salt, lard size of a walnut, moulded with flour.   Mould well.—Mrs. J. M. Raymond.

BROWN BREAD.

One quart corn meal, one pint flour, one cup molasses, one cup yeast, one teaspoon soda, one tablespoon salt, four cups cold water. Mix well the meal, flour and salt, make a hole in the middle, put in the molasses, yeast and soda, stir it well, then add the water a cupful at a time. Steam six or seven hours, bake two hours.—Mrs. C. H. BAILEY.

JOHNNY CAKE.

Two coffee cups meal, one and one-half coffee cups flour, two eggs, one teaspoon soda, sour milk. Stir well.—Mrs. H. D. LEONARD.

Salads.

CABBAGE SALAD.

One medium head cabbage, three eggs beaten, six table-spoons cream, and three of melted butter, (or five tablespoons milk and four of butter), one teaspoon or more of mustard, one of pepper, one of salt, one coffee-cup strong vinegar heated until it thickens but not boils. Mix with the cabbage when hot. Cover tightly.—Mrs. H. D. Leonard.

CHICKEN SALAD.

One chicken, smothered; when cold, cut in small pieces; do not use a chopping knife. Prepare as much celery as chicken, two medium-sized cucumber pickles cut up; also, the whites of the eggs left from the dressing. This part of salad may be mixed at once, as it does not hurt to stand, and the dressing poured over just before it is used.

DRESSING.

Yolks of four hard-boiled eggs mashed to a smooth paste, one-half teaspoon salt, one-half teaspoon pepper, two of mustard, two of sugar, four of salad-oil, one small teacup of good vinegar. Pour over chicken, and mix with a fork; do not stir it. This is enough for eight persons.—Mrs. J. B. Henslee.

COLD SLAW.

One small head of cabbage and one onion, chopped fine; add one teaspoon salt, two tablespoons sugar, one cup vinegar, and a little pepper.—Mrs. Hugh Parry.

COLD SLAW.

One-third pint vinegar, three tablespoons sugar, two of cream, one of butter, two eggs beaten with cream. Cook vinegar, sugar and butter together; when boiling, add eggs and cream, cooking until thick. Chop the cabbage fine, adding celery, if obtainable; if not, celery salt; then pour over it the dressing.—MRS. O. H. SIMONS.

POTATO SALAD.

Pare six or eight large potatoes, boil until done, and slice thin while hot. Peel and cut up a white onion in small bits and mix with the potatoes. Cut up some breakfast bacon in small bits, sufficient to fill a teacup, and fry it a light brown. Remove the meat, and into the grease stir three tablespoons vinegar, making a sour gravy, which, with the bacon, pour over the potato and onion. Mix lightly. To be eaten when hot.—MRS. McKENZIE.

WINTER SALAD.

Two boiled potatoes pressed through a sieve, one spoonful mustard, two of salt, three of olive oil, one of vinegar, yolks of two hard-boiled eggs, a little onion chopped fine, one spoonful anchovy sauce added last.—MRS. H. D. LEONARD.

CABBAGE SLAW.

Boil one cup of vinegar, melt in it a piece of butter the size of a walnut. Beat together one egg, one teaspoon each mustard, sugar, salt, and half teaspoon pepper. Pour the boiling vinegar on this mixture. Stir it well, then put back on the stove and boil one minute. Pour this on the cabbage.—MRS. McKENZIE.

SALAD DRESSING.

Yolks of three eggs, two teaspoons wet mustard, one-half cup vinegar, two tablespoons sugar, one-half teaspoon salt, two teaspoons butter. Heat vinegar and butter, add other ingredients, and cook until thick as cream.—MRS. H. C. DIMICK.

CARROT SALAD.

Select tender, rich colored carrots, scrape and boil them in fast-boiling water until tender; cut in thin slices and put in a glass salad bowl. Sprinkle with sifted loaf sugar, add the juice of a large, fresh lemon, and a wineglass of olive oil. Garnish the dish with very thin slices of onion, or any fresh, green salad leaves.—MRS. JOHN ALFRED.

EGG SALAD.

Six hard-boiled eggs cut quite fine, one-fourth of a cabbage chopped. Mix well together.

DRESSING.

Three tablespoons of melted butter, one small teaspoon each of pepper and salt, one teaspoon of prepared mustard. Mix together and pour over salad.—MRS. C. A. FREAR.

SALAD DRESSING.

Yolks of two eggs, or one whole egg, well beaten, added to five tablespoons boiling vinegar. Add butter the size of an egg. Cook in a pan of boiling water. When cool, season to taste with salt, pepper and mustard. Thin with sweet cream to the required consistency.—MRS. H. D. LEONARD.

POTATO SALAD.

Boil ten or twelve medium-sized potatoes, not too soft, cool a little, peel and slice; add pepper and salt, two tablespoons vinegar (be careful with vinegar not to make it too sour), two tablespoons hot water, a little onion cut very fine. Let it stand half an hour; then add two or three spoons olive oil. Mix well, then serve. To be eaten with cold meats.—MRS. WERNER.

EGG SALAD.

Two dozen eggs, boiled hard and chopped not too fine, equal quantity of celery. Mix with Durkee's Salad Dressing to taste. Garnish the dish with lettuce and serve. This is sufficient for ten or twelve persons.

CABBAGE SLAW.

Take a medium head cabbage, chop fine, with one tablespoon of salt; squeeze the water out thoroughly with your hands, then pour one-half cup vinegar over.

DRESSING.

Three eggs, one-fourth cup butter, two tablespoons condensed milk. Season with pepper. Beat together with one-half teacup boiling water; cook five minutes and pour over the cabbage. It is then ready to serve.—Mrs. P. B. Turnbull.

Pies.

MINCE PIES.

Four pounds of beef, twelve pounds of apples, one-half pound salt pork, two pounds of sugar, four pounds of raisins, one pound of citron, four ounces of cassia, two of nutmeg, one of cloves, one pint molasses, one quart of boiled cider, or one quart of good vinegar.—Mrs. Taylor.

MOCK MINCE PIES.

Five large crackers rolled fine, one and a half cups molasses, one-half cup sugar, two-thirds cup vinegar, two cups chopped raisins, one-half cup butter, one and a half cups cold water, a little salt, one teaspoon each all kinds of spices. Put all together and cook until thick. This will make four pies.—Mrs. L. A. Grover.

LEMON PIE.

One heaping tablespoon cornstarch, dissolved in a little cold water; pour on one coffee-cup boiling water, and boil until it puffs up; take off the stove and add two-thirds coffee-cup sugar, yolks of two eggs, small lump of butter, and juice and grated rind of two lemons.—Mrs. O. H. Simons.

PIE - CRUST.

Four cups of flour, one large teaspoon salt, one teaspoon baking powder, one scant cup lard, one large cup water. Mix rather soft. Take part of crust and roll in butter for top crust.—Miss Price.

H. M. BLAKELY

WILL BE FOUND AT

No. 140 East Sixth Street,

AFTER MAY 15th, 1889,

WITH A FULL LINE OF

Dry * Goods

AND NOTIONS.

CREAM PIE.

Whip one quart of stiff cream, add sugar and vanilla to your taste. Line pie-plates with crust, and prick with a fork before baking. When cool, fill with the whipped cream.—MRS. PAXTON.

LEMON PIE.

Grate the rind of one lemon, add one tablespoon cornstarch dissolved in a little cold water, one teacup boiling water, one whole egg and the yolks of two. Take the whites of two eggs for the meringue, and brown in the oven.—MRS. HUGH PARRY.

SWEET POTATO PIE.

Boil or bake sufficient sweet potatoes to make a pint of pulp when rubbed through a colander; add a pint of milk, a small cup of sugar, a little salt, yolks of two eggs, one teaspoon lemon extract. Bake in a shallow pan lined with rich crust. When done, beat the whites with a little powdered sugar for top, and brown in the oven.—MRS. HUGH PARRY.

?LEMON PIE.

The juice and grated rind of one lemon, one tablespoon cornstarch, one teacup sugar, two eggs (reserving the white of one), one cup boiling water. Mix all together and cook, stirring constantly until it thickens; pour it in the crust and bake. Beat the white with three spoons sugar and spread on top; return to the oven and brown lightly.—MRS. MCKENZIE.

CREAM PIE.

One pint of milk put in a steamer; let it come to a boil; then add half a cup of sugar, two tablespoons cornstarch and yolks of two eggs well beaten together. Flavor with lemon. When cool, have crust baked ready for filling. Beat the whites of the eggs, spread on top and brown in the oven.—MRS. HUGH PARRY.

ENGLISH APPLE PIE.

Small piece of butter in pan, add apple sauce, then cover with crust and bake; add apple and crust and bake again, and so on until pan is filled. Serve with hot sauce.—MRS. PAXTON.

CREAM PIE.

One cup sugar, one egg, one-fourth cup butter, one-half cup sweet milk, two cups flour, one teaspoon soda, one-half teaspoon of essence of bitter almonds. This makes two cakes, baked in round shallow tins.

CREAM FOR FILLING.

One scant pint milk, one cup sugar, yolks of two eggs, one-half cup flour. Flavor with vanilla. Boil the milk, add flour moistened smoothly with cold milk, then sugar and eggs; let it boil to the consistency of cream. Use the whites of the eggs with two tablespoons sugar for the meringue. Cut open the warm cakes, put cream between and meringue on top. Brown the two pies in the oven.—MRS. HUGH PARRY.

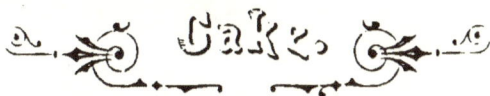

Cake.

WHITE CAKE.

Whites of eight eggs well beaten, one and a third cups sugar, one scant half cup butter, three cups sifted flour, one cup sweet milk, one-half teaspoon baking powder mixed in the flour. Mix butter and sugar, then stir in gradually milk and flour, sifting the flour in, then the whites of eggs. Flavor with lemon.—Mrs. J. B. HENSLEE.

GINGER COOKIES.

Two cups molasses, one cup sugar, one cup water, one large cup butter, one tablespoon soda, one tablespoon ginger, little cinnamon. Flour enough to roll.—Mrs. Wm. PEMBERTHY.

CHEAP CREAM CAKE.

One cup sugar, one cup sweet milk, two cups flour, one egg, one tablespoon butter, one teaspoon baking powder. Flavor to taste. Bake in layers.

FILLING.

One egg, one-half cup sugar, one-fourth cup flour mixed with a little cold milk, and stirred into one cup boiling milk. Boil until thick enough. Flavor.—Miss CORA PADDOCK.

TEA CAKE.

One cup sugar, one tablespoon butter, two eggs well beaten, one cup sweet milk, one and a half teaspoons baking powder. Flour enough for pretty thick batter. One teaspoon lemon or vanilla extract. Bake in hot gem pans.—Miss F. L. RAYMOND.

GINGERBREAD.

One cup molasses, one egg, butter size of an egg, three cups of flour, one-fourth teaspoon cloves, one-half teaspoon ginger and one of soda. Beat molasses, egg, butter and part of flour together; pour a cup of boiling water on soda, add it to mixture, then remainder of flour, beating thoroughly.—Mrs. O. H. Simons

COOKIES.

One cup butter, two cups sugar, one cup sweet cream. Melt the sugar and pour over the butter. Stir while it melts. After it is cold, cream it and stir in the sweet cream; after putting in the cream and mixing thoroughly, add an even teaspoon of soda. Beat three eggs, yolks and whites together, and put in, but do not mix until you have added some flour. Mix them as soft as possible, taking them up from the table with a knife. The less flour the better. Use extra C sugar; you cannot use granulated sugar.—Mrs. S. J. Hanna.

ANGEL FOOD.

The whites of eleven eggs beaten to a stiff froth, a tumbler and a half each of flour and pulverized sugar. Sift the sugar and flour twice, adding a teaspoon of cream tartar, and a little salt. Stir lightly, flavor to taste. Bake twenty-five minutes. Do not grease the pan.—Mrs. C. E. Dodge.

CHEAP SPONGE CAKE.

One-half large teacup sugar, one teacup flour, three eggs, two tablespoons milk, one heaping teaspoon baking powder, one teaspoon essence of lemon. Stir all well together.—Mrs. H. D. Leonard.

JENNIE'S SUGAR CAKES.

Three cups sugar, two of butter, three eggs well beaten, one teaspoon soda. Flour sufficient to roll out.—Mrs. A. J. Lampshire.

NUT CAKE.

Six eggs, one large cup of sugar, one-half cup butter, one-half cup sweet milk, one pound of English walnuts rolled fine, one tablespoon of baking powder, and flour to thicken. Flavor with extract of strawberry, and bake in a flat pan.

COOKED FROSTING.

The whites of three eggs beaten stiff, and one cup of granulated sugar. Put sugar in a pan and cover with water, let it cook until it will hair from the end of a fork. Stir the beaten eggs with this until perfectly cold; it will then be thick enough to spread on cake.—Mrs. W. L. Scott.

COOKIES.

Two cups sugar, three-fourths cup butter, one and a half cups sour milk, one teaspoon soda. Flavor with nutmeg. Flour enough to roll softly. Sprinkle sugar on top, cut and bake.—Mrs. P. B. Turnbull.

CHEAP FRUIT CAKE.

Three eggs, two-thirds cup brown sugar, fill up the cup with molasses, half cup butter, half cup sour milk, three cups sifted flour, one teaspoon each of cinnamon, cloves and soda, half teaspoon nutmeg. Add currants and raisins.—Mrs. H. D. Leonard.

LEMON FILLING FOR CAKE.

The juice of two lemons, two eggs, piece of butter the size of a hickory nut, coffee-cup of sugar. Beat all together and boil until it thickens, stirring carefully. This is enough for four layers.—Mrs. C. E. Dodge.

COOKIES.

One cup light brown sugar, one-half cup butter, one egg, two tablespoons sweet milk, and two teaspoons of baking powder. Add flower enough to roll thin. Bake in a quick oven.—Mrs. John Alfred.

MARBLE CAKE.

For the white cake: One cup butter, three cups white sugar, five even cups flour, one-half cup sweet milk, one-half teaspoon of soda, whites of eight eggs. Flavor with lemon.

For the dark cake: One cup butter, two cups of brown sugar, one cup of molasses, one cup sour milk, one teaspoon soda, four cups of flour, yolks of eight eggs and one whole egg, spices of all kinds. Put in pans first a layer of dark, then a layer of white, and so on, finishing with a dark layer.—MRS. WM. MORRIS.

FRUIT CAKE.

One pound of flour, one of brown sugar, three-fourths pound butter, twelve eggs, one and a half pounds raisins, one and one-half pounds currants, one-half pound citron, one-half pound almonds, one-half pound figs, one-half pint sour milk, one level teaspoon soda, two teaspoons each of allspice, cloves and cinnamon, one teaspoon mace.—MRS. C. A. FREAR.

WHITE CAKE.

One cup pulverized sugar, and one-half cup white butter beaten to a cream, one-half cup milk, one and two-thirds cups flour, one-fourth cup cornstarch, whites of nine eggs beaten to a froth, one teaspoon of baking powder and lemon extract.—MRS. G. B. HARKER.

DOUGHNUTS.

One coffee-cup granulated sugar, one-fourth coffee-cup butter, one coffee-cup milk, four eggs, two tablespoons water, two teaspoons baking powder, one teaspoon salt, one nutmeg. Cream the sugar and butter as for cake, add the eggs, well beaten, then milk, water, salt and nutmeg; next flour enough to make stiff for handling. Do not roll out all at once, but keep adding a little fresh every time, and roll half an inch thick. Add baking powder with the flour and have your lard just right. In about an hour after cooking, roll in powdered sugar. Keep well covered in an earthen jar.—MRS. GUILBAULT.

JELLY ROLL.

Two teacups of coffee sugar, two teacups of sifted flour, two heaping teaspoons baking powder; into this break six good-sized eggs and beat all well together. Turn into square tins and bake in a quick oven to a light brown. When done, turn out on a moulding board, and spread with jelly. Roll carefully, and wrap each roll in a clean napkin. Can be used for table at once.—Mrs. Hugh Parry.

LEMON CAKE.

One cup sugar, one-half cup butter beaten to a cream ; then add the yolks and whites of five eggs, beaten separately. Grate the rind of one lemon, add the juice of same, and three-fourths cup sweet milk. Dissolve one-half teaspoon of soda and stir all together. Do not mix too stiff. Bake in a moderate oven. —Mrs. F. M. Mahn.

PRINCE OF WALES CAKE.

White Part.—One cup sugar, one-half cup butter, whites of three eggs, two cups flour, one-half cup sweet milk, one teaspoon baking powder.

Dark Part.—One cup brown sugar, one-half cup butter, yolks of three eggs, one-half cup sweet milk, two cups flour, one cup seeded raisins, tablespoon cinnamon, little nutmeg, one teaspoon baking powder. Bake in jelly tins, two white and two dark.

Cooked icing to be put between the layers. One and a half cups sugar, whites of two eggs ; dissolve the sugar in water and boil until it hairs on the end of the spoon ; beat the eggs to a stiff froth, and stir it in the hot syrup, and beat until cold.— Mrs. P. B. Turnbull..

DROP GINGER CAKES.

One quart flour, half pint milk, half pint molasses, two teaspoons soda, two teaspoons ginger, butter size of an egg. Drop with spoon on tins.—Mrs. H. D. Leonard.

MARBLE CHOCOLATE CAKE.

Light Part.—One cup sugar, one-half cup butter, whites three eggs, one cup milk, one teaspoon baking powder, about two cups flour.

Dark Part —One cup sugar, one-half cup butter, yolks three eggs, one cup milk, three-fourths cup grated chocolate, moistened with boiling water, one teaspoon baking powder, about two cups flour. Flavor with vanilla. Put alternate spoonfulls of the batter in a round deep pan with a stem, and bake until done.—Mrs. P. B. Turnbull.

GINGERBREAD.

One cup brown sugar, one cup New Orleans molasses, one cup shortening, three eggs, one cup sour milk, teaspoon soda, pinch of salt, tablespoon ginger, little cinnamon. To be eaten as a dessert with cream.—Mrs. Guilbault.

GOLD CAKE.

Two heaping cups flour, yolks of four eggs, one cup sugar, one and a half cups butter, one and a half cups sweet milk, one and a half teaspoons soda, one teaspoon cream tartar. Flavor to taste.—Mrs. M. L. Clark.

CORNSTARCH CAKE.

Whites of three eggs, one and a half cups cornstarch, one and a half cups milk, one cup pulverized sugar, one and a half cups butter, one and a half teaspoons cream tartar, one-fourth teaspoon soda. Flavor with lemon.—Mrs. M. L. Clark.

WHITE CAKE.

One cup sugar, one-half cup butter, two cups flour, whites of seven eggs, and a scant teaspoon baking powder. Cream the butter and sugar, and add gradually the well-beaten whites, with a half teacup of sweet milk. Flour and extract to taste. Bake in a moderate oven, well covered, until light.—Mrs. Cooper.

SPONGE ROLL.

One cup sugar, two cups flour, six eggs, six teaspoons of water, and one of baking powder. Beat the eggs and sugar very light, add the rest of the ingredients and beat rapidly until smooth. Bake quickly; turn on a clean cloth, spread with jelly or any kind of filling that is liked, and roll while warm. This mixture can be baked in jelly tins, if preferred.—Mrs. COOPER.

ROLLED JELLY CAKE.

Four eggs, whites and yolks beaten separately, one-half cup of pulverized sugar, one cup flour, one teaspoon baking powder. Flavor with lemon extract. Bake in a large flat tin.—Mrs. P. B. TURNBULL.

SPONGE CAKE.

One heaping coffee-cup flour, one even coffee-cup sugar, six eggs, essence lemon.—Mrs. H. D. LEONARD.

COOKIES.

Two cups granulated sugar, one cup butter, three eggs, one cup boiling water, one teaspoon baking powder, one teaspoon soda. Flour enough to roll good. Flavor with nutmeg to suit the taste.—Mrs. G. B. HARKER.

COFFEE CAKE.

Four eggs (reserve the whites of two for frosting), one and one-half cups molasses, the same of sugar, two cups chopped raisins, one-half cup butter, one cup strong cold coffee, one teaspoon salt, two teaspoons soda, one teaspoon each all kinds spices. Mix stiff with flour. This will make two large loaves.—Mrs. L. A. GROVER.

DOUGHNUTS.

One cup sweet milk, one even cup sugar, two eggs, one teaspoon salt, two teaspoons baking powder, two teaspoons melted butter, flour to roll.—Mrs. J. M. RAYMOND.

BRIDE'S CAKE.

Whites of twelve eggs, three cups sugar, small cup butter, cup sweet milk, four small cups of flour, half cup cornstarch, two teaspoons baking powder. Flavor to taste.

A cup of thin sliced citron dusted with flour, added to the above, makes a very nice citron cake.—MRS. A. J. LAMPSHIRE.

WHITE CAKE.

Whites of four eggs, one cup sugar, good half cup butter, cup of milk, three cups of flour, one teaspoon baking powder, one teaspoon of flavoring.

The yolks of the eggs, and the same ingredients make a nice gold cake.—MRS. McKENZIE.

HARRISON CAKE.

One cup sugar, one-half cup butter, three eggs well beaten, half teaspoon soda stirred in half cup sour milk, two small cups flour. Flavor with lemon or vanilla. Pour in small dripping pan. Bake half an hour.—MISS R. H. NASH.

SPONGE CAKE.

One cup sugar, two scant cups flour, one-half cup cold water, five eggs beaten separately, one teaspoon baking powder, one teaspoon extract.—MRS. T. KYLE.

FIG FILLING FOR CAKE.

One and a half pounds figs chopped fine; boil down with half a cup of water. Cool, then fill the cake.—MRS. GUILBAULT.

FRUIT COOKIES.

Two eggs, one and a third cups brown sugar, two-thirds cup warm water, two-thirds cup butter, even teaspoon soda dissolved in hot water, one cup chopped raisins; salt, cinnamon and cloves. Flour enough to handle easily.—MRS. C. A. FREAR.

CHOCOLATE FROSTING.

Shave three fourths cup Baker's chocolate, add three-fourths cup sugar beaten with one egg and a tablespoon of cream. Cook over the tea kettle.—Miss Price.

CHEAP DROP CAKES.

One cup molasses, one cup water, three cups flour, two eggs, one teaspoon soda, butter size of an egg, one teaspoon each cloves, allspice and cinnamon.—Mrs. C. H. Bailey.

WHITE CAKE.

One cup sugar, one-half cup butter, whites of nine eggs, two and three-fourths cups flour, one-fourth cup cornstarch, one cup milk, one teaspoon baking powder. Flavor with lemon. Beat sugar, butter, flour and milk together, then add eggs and baking powder.—Mrs. C. A. Frear.

SPICE CAKE.

Yolks of five eggs, one cup sugar, one cup milk, two and a half cups flour, one teaspoon baking powder, butter the size of an egg, a heaping teaspoon of all kinds of spices.—Mrs. C. E. Dodge.

ANGEL FOOD.

Whites of ten eggs, three-fourths tumbler pulverized sugar, one full tumbler of flour measured and then sifted seven times, three-fourths teaspoon cream tartar sifted in the flour. Lemon extract or bitter almond.—Mrs. T. Kyle.

GINGER SNAPS.

Mix three teaspoons baking powder with one and a quarter quarts of flour; add to this one-quarter pound sugar, two teaspoons butter, one-half pint molasses, and two tablespoons extract of ginger. Roll very thin and bake in a few minutes. Will soften by being kept.—Mrs. John Alfred.

PLAIN CAKE FOR LAYERS.

One-half cup butter, three-fourths cup sugar, two eggs, one cup milk, two and a half cups flour after sifting three times, one teaspoon baking powder. Mix butter and yolks thoroughly, add milk, flour and baking powder; lastly, the beaten whites, with a good amount of flavoring.

CREAM FOR LAYER CAKE.

Yolks of two eggs, one tablespoon sugar, one teaspoon flour and one teacup milk; boil until it thickens.—Mrs. O. H. Simons.

WHITE CAKE.

Whites of two eggs beaten to a stiff froth, one cup sugar, piece of butter the size of an egg, one cup milk, two and a half cups flour, teaspoon baking powder. Flavor to taste.—Mrs. C. E. Dodge.

MARBLE CAKE.

Light Part.—Whites of four eggs, cup of sugar, one-half cup butter, one-half cup sweet milk, one teaspoon baking powder, two and a half cups flour. Flavor with lemon.

Dark Part.—Yolks of four eggs, cup brown sugar, half cup molasses, half cup butter, half cup sour milk, teaspoon soda, two and a half cups flour.

Stir together, dark and light parts, and bake two hours in a slow oven.—Mrs. Taylor.

DOUGHNUTS.

One cup sour milk, cup and a half C sugar, two teaspoons melted butter, half a teaspoon soda, pinch of salt, flour enough to mix soft dough. Cinnamon to taste.—Mrs. Hugh Parry.

POUND CAKE.

One and three-fourths cups sugar, half pound butter rubbed to a cream, one pound flour sifted three times, whites of sixteen eggs, one cup walnuts, one teaspoon baking powder.—Mrs. Werner.

CREAM CAKE.

Whites of three eggs beaten very light, one-fourth cup butter and one cup sugar beaten to a cream, one cup milk, three cups flour, two spoons baking powder. Stir eggs in last and bake in layers.

For the cream, take the yolks of two eggs, one cup milk, one-half cup sugar, two tablespoons cornstarch, butter size of a hickory-nut. Beat the yolks, then add the other ingredients and boil. Flavor to taste when cool. Do not spread on layers until cool.—Mrs. John Alfred.

RAISIN CAKE.

Take one and a quarter pounds of light dough, a teacup of sugar, one of butter, three eggs, a teaspoon of soda, one pound of raisins, nutmeg or cinnamon to the taste. Bake one hour. Let it rise before being baked.—Mrs. John Alfred.

COOKIES.

Cup of melted butter, two-thirds cup sour milk, teaspoon soda dissolved in hot water, three eggs well beaten, one and a fourth cups sugar, flour to roll thin, and bake in a quick oven.—Mrs. J. M. Raymond.

BANANA CAKE.

Two cups sugar, one cup butter, one cup sweet milk, three cups flour, yolks of five eggs, whites of three, two teaspoons baking powder. Bake in layers.

Filling.—Whites of two eggs, one-half pound powdered sugar; spread each layer with the icing. Cut banana thin with silver knife and spread thick over icing. Strawberries may be used the same way.—Mrs. Werner.

STRAWBERRY SHORT CAKE.

One cup sour milk, very small teaspoon soda, one tablespoon melted butter, little salt, add flour to thicken, and bake in pie tins. Split the cakes and add berries.—Mrs. Guilbault.

SPONGE CAKE.

Two cups flour, two teaspoons baking powder, six eggs, one cup milk, two cups sugar.—Mrs. John Alfred.

GINGER SNAPS.

One cup C sugar, one-half cup molasses, one cup boiling water, two eggs, one teaspoon each soda, ginger and cinnamon. Flour enough to roll out well.—Mrs. G. B. Harker.

DOUGHNUTS.

One coffee cup of not too thick sour cream, or one of sour milk and one tablespoon butter, two eggs, a little nutmeg and salt, one teacup sugar, one small teaspoon soda dissolved. Mix soft.—Mrs. A. J. Lampshire.

OLD-FASHIONED GINGERBREAD.

One tablespoon soda, one teaspoon pulverized alum, each in one-half cup boiling water. Add one pint New Orleans molasses, one tablespoon ginger, one-half cup butter. Mix soft, roll thin, and bake in a quick oven.—Mrs. Hugh Parry.

CONFECTIONERY FROSTING.

Take the white of one egg (don't beat it) and stir powdered sugar into it until it is as thick as cold cream, or as thick as it can be spread on the cake. Flavor if desired.

LAYER CAKE.

TWO CAKES OF THREE LAYERS.

One cup sugar, one-half cup butter, four eggs, one cup milk, four cups flour, two heaping teaspoons baking powder.

CREAM FILLING.

One cup milk, half cup sugar; boil one minute. Two heaping tablespoons cornstarch, yolks of two eggs; boil five minutes. When cold add one teaspoon vanilla.

COOKIES.

One cup C sugar, one cup melted lard, two teaspoons baking powder, one egg; flour enough to roll without sticking.—Mrs. Hugh Parry.

ICE-CREAM CAKE.

Two cups sugar, scant cup of butter, one cup sweet milk, two cups flour, one cup cornstarch, whites of eight eggs, two teaspoons baking powder sifted in the flour and cornstarch. Cream, butter and sugar, add milk, then flour and cornstarch, and last eggs well beaten. Bake in layers.

ICING FOR THE ABOVE.

Whites of four eggs, four cups sugar; pour half pint boiling water on sugar and boil till it candies; pour boiling sugar on the well beaten whites; then beat till it is cold. Flavor with lemon and two teaspoons vanilla. Spread between the cake.—Mrs. Werner.

GINGER SNAPS.

Bring to a scald one cup of molasses, and stir in one tablespoon soda; pour it while foaming over one cup sugar, one egg and one tablespoon ginger beaten together; then add one tablespoon vinegar and flour enough to roll, stirred in as lightly as possible.—Mrs. Wm. Morris.

VARIETY CAKE.

Light Part.—Whites of three eggs, one cup sugar, butter size of an egg, half cup sweet milk, one teaspoon baking powder. Flavor with lemon. About two cups flour.

Dark Part.—One-half cup sugar, one-half cup molasses, cup of chopped raisins, yolks of three eggs, one-half teaspoon soda, half a cup of coffee, about two cups flour, spices of all kinds. Bake in square tins. Beat the whites of two eggs with a little sugar, flavor with lemon; this is to be used between the layers, then add enough sugar to frost the top.—Mrs. Hugh Parry.

COOKIES.

Rub together till white one teacup butter and two of sugar; beat two eggs and stir into the mixture with a little flour. Grate in a nutmeg. Dissolve one teaspoon soda in one cup milk. Add flour to roll easy.—Mrs. H. D. Leonard.

MACAROONS.

One-half pound grated almonds, one-half pound sugar, one lemon, whites of two eggs. Blanch and chop the almonds, add eggs and sugar, with the juice of lemon. Drop a small quantity on paper greased on the back, which will enable you to take off the pan.—Mrs. Werner.

COOKIES.

One-half cup cold water, one teacup white sugar, one-half cup butter, one-half cup sweet cream, three eggs, two heaping teaspoons baking powder, one teaspoon lemon extract. Mix well and roll to about one-fourth an inch in thickness. Sprinkle with granulated sugar, cut, and bake in a quick oven.—Mrs. Wm. Morris.

CREAM PUFFS.

One pint of flour, one large pint of water, one-half pound of melted butter; let the butter stand a few moments till the salt settles to the bottom; eight eggs, grated rind of half a lemon. Set the butter and water on the stove to boil; when it boils add the flour and stir quickly till it comes off from the dish; let it cool, then beat the eggs in one at a time. Drop from the spoon on buttered pans, not too near together. Bake in a quick oven. Sprinkle the puffs with powdered sugar and fill with cream. This will make forty-five puffs.—Mrs. Werner.

CHOCOLATE ICING.

One tablespoon melted chocolate. One and a half cups sugar boiled to a syrup in two tablespoons water. Add to this while hot the whites of two eggs, and then stir in chocolate.

"BATAVIA"

Canned Goods are Unequalled!

EVERYTHING PACKED UNDER THIS BRAND IS FREE
FROM ALL ADULTERATION, AND PUT UP
WITH CARE AND CLEANLINESS.

THE FOLLOWING VARIETIES, 1889 PACK, WILL BE IN STOCK
THIS SEASON, AND CAN BE OBTAINED
OF YOUR GROCER:

Blackberries,
Blueberries,
Preserved White Pitted Cherries,
Preserved Red Pitted Cherries,
Spiced Red Pitted Cherries,
Red Pitted Pie Cherries,
Preserved Red Currants,
Yellow Crawford Peaches,
Grated Pineapple,
Sliced Pineapple,
Red Antwerp Raspberries,
Black Raspberries,
Preserved Gooseberries,

Preserved Strawberries,
Extra Strawberries,

Asparagus,
Lima Beans,
Stringless Beans,
Sugar Corn,
Extra Fine Peas,
Early June Peas,
Marrowfat Peas,
Succotash,
Tomatoes.

STRICTLY PURE MAPLE SYRUP,

Canned at the Sugar Bush, thereby retaining its Original Flavor and
Purity. Note the brand, "BATAVIA."

Take no other under the supposition that you are getting some-
thing equal to the "BATAVIA." If your grocer does not keep
"BATAVIA" goods, he can obtain them from

THE C. S. MOREY MERCANTILE CO.

Wholesale Grocers,

Sole Agents for Colorado.   DENVER, COLO.

JELLY OR CHOCOLATE LAYER CAKE.

Four eggs, *small* cup sugar, *one and a* half a cups of flour, in which a teaspoon of baking powder has been well mixed, pinch of salt, half cup of milk or cream put in the last thing.—MRS. WERNER.

CINNAMON CAKE.

One and a fourth pounds flour, one pound sugar, four eggs, half pound butter, half pound grated almonds, one teaspoon cinnamon, grated rind of one lemon. Stir sugar and eggs for half an hour, then add the butter, almonds, cinnamon, lemon rind and flour. Roll out to the thickness of one-fourth an inch or less. Cut out with cake-cutter and stand over night, and bake the next morning in a moderate oven.—MRS. WERNER.

SUET PUDDING.

Cup chopped suet, cup molasses, cup sweet milk, three cups flour after it is sifted, cup stoned raisins and a few whole ones, teaspoon soda dissolved in a little boiling water, teaspoon each of cloves and cinnamon, one-half teaspoon nutmeg. Steam until done, at least three hours.

SAUCE FOR SAME.

Butter size of an egg, cup of sugar, tablespoon flour. Put all together and pour on boiling water, cook one-half hour. Flavor with brandy, or anything preferred.—Mrs. S. J. Hanna.

SNOW PUDDING.

One-half box Nelson's gelatine, one pint boiling water, one and a half cups sugar, juice of two lemons. When mixture is cool add beaten whites of eight eggs, and beat until ready to congeal. Tint with fruit coloring, and serve with whipped cream. —Mrs. J. B. Henslee.

TAPIOCA PUDDING.

Take one-half cup of tapioca, soak over night, put on the stove in the morning; cook up clear, add one cup of sugar, large spoon of butter and raisins. Bake one hour, set away until cool. Serve with cream.—Mrs. Hugh Parry.

PLUM PUDDING.

Six crackers pounded fine, six eggs, one quart boiling milk, one cup sugar, one-half cup butter. Raisins, currants, citron and spices to taste.—Mrs. W. H. Nash.

POP-OVERS.

Three eggs, three cups flour, three cups milk, a little salt, butter the size of an egg, one heaping teaspoon baking powder. Beat the whites separate and add last. Bake in small muffin tins in a quick oven.—Mrs. Hugh Parry.

PLUM PUDDING.

Chop and rub to a cream one-fourth pound of suet, add scant half pound sugar ; mix well. Add four well beaten eggs, one grated nutmeg, one-half teaspoon each cloves, mace, and salt, one-half cup brandy, three-fourths cup milk, flour to make a thin batter. Seed and chop one-half pound raisins, wash clean one-half pound currants, cut into thin slices one-half pound citron. Sprinkle fruits with flour to prevent their settling to the bottom of batter. Steam five or eight hours.

SAUCE FOR PUDDING.

Cream two cups of butter, add slowly one cup powdered sugar, the unbeaten white of one egg, two tablespoons of wine and one of brandy, one-fourth cup boiling water. Heat until smooth and creamy. Heat the bowl for the creamed butter, and when adding wine do so slowly to prevent curdling. This pudding will keep for a year. As it can be prepared beforehand, it is excellent for Christmas, saving much labor on that busy day.—Mrs. H. C. Dimick.

CHOCOLATE PUDDING.

One quart milk, three squares Baker's chocolate melted in the milk, two eggs, four large spoons cornstarch, three large spoons sugar. Beat sugar, eggs and cornstarch together, add small teaspoon salt. Cool in a mould. Serve with whipped cream.—Mrs. F. G. Barker.

INDIAN PUDDING.

One quart milk, one cup white meal or gold dust, one cup sugar, two eggs. Salt. Scald the meal in milk, and bake about two hours slowly.

QUEEN OF PUDDINGS.

One pint bread crumbs, one quart of new milk, one cup sugar, yolks of four eggs. Bake in slow oven; when done spread with jelly. Whip whites of eggs to stiff froth, add four tablespoons pulverized sugar, spread on top, return to oven and brown. Serve with whipped cream.—Mrs. H. C. Dimick.

SNOW PUDDING.

One-half package gelatine, soak two hours in one pint cold water; heat without boiling until it is all dissolved; when nearly cold, beat thoroughly with an egg beater, then add the whites of four eggs beaten to a stiff froth, one cup powdered sugar, the juice and grated rind of one lemon. Let it cool. Use the yolks for a soft custard to put around each dish when served.—Mrs. T. Kyle.

TRANSCENDENTAL PUDDING.

Half a teacup of rice steamed in one quart of milk two hours. Take the yolks of three eggs, grated rind of one lemon, a little salt, sweeten to taste. This is to be stirred into the rice. Butter the pudding dish. Bake. Beat the whites stiff, sweeten with pulverized sugar, flavor with the juice of the lemon. Set in oven and brown lightly.—Mrs. H. D. Leonard.

SNOW PUDDING.

Pour half a pint boiling water over half a box gelatine; stir until dissolved. Into this squeeze the juice of three lemons, add two cups sugar; beat whites of four eggs to a stiff froth, add gradually to the dissolved gelatine, etc. Beat constantly thirty minutes, until it has the appearance of snow. Dip moulds in cold water, and put the mixture on ice to cool.

CUSTARD FOR THE ABOVE.

Three cups milk, three-fourths cup sugar, yolks of four eggs. Flavor with vanilla. Boil the milk and stir in the eggs gradually, being careful not to let it lump.—Mrs. H. C. Dimick.

BAKED CUSTARD.

Scald one quart of milk, then add four well-beaten eggs; sweeten and flavor to taste. Pour into a pudding dish, and set in a pan of hot water in the oven.

ORANGE PUDDING.

Peel four oranges, slice very thin, lay in a deep dish with one cup white sugar strewn over it; set it away for an hour.

CREAM FOR SAME.

One-half cup flour, three-fourths cup sugar, small piece of butter, yolks three eggs, one half teaspoon essence lemon. Beat these together and pour into one pint boiling water; let it boil a few minutes; pour over the oranges while hot. Beat the whites of the eggs to a stiff froth, add two teaspoons sugar, spread over the top, place in the oven to brown a few minutes. Serve cold.— Mrs. W. H. Nash.

BAKED CUSTARD.

Beat the yolks of four eggs half an hour; add five ounces pulverized sugar, then one quart cold, new milk; add a teaspoon lemon extract, fill the cups and set them in a pan half filled with *warm* water. Place the pan in a rather cool oven and gradually increase the heat. In about twenty minutes dip a teaspoon in one of the custards to see if it is firm. Great care is needed in baking custards, for if left in the oven a minute too long, or if the fire is too hot, the milk will certainly whey.—Mrs. Wm. Morris.

DANDY PUDDING.

One quart sweet milk, two tablespoons cornstarch, five tablespoons sugar, yolks of four eggs. Beat the cornstarch and sugar together, and stir into the milk when boiling; stir until it thickens and is smooth. Flavor with a teaspoon vanilla. Butter the pudding dish. Beat the whites of the eggs to a stiff froth with a little pulverized sugar, pour on the top, put in the oven and bake.—Mrs. H. D. Leonard.

Dessert.

APPLE MERINGUE.

Pare and stew a few apples just as you would for sauce; take two or three slices of bread, butter them well. Line a bread pan with pie crust, cover with a layer of the apple sauce well sweetened with sugar, next a layer of bread, then of apples. Bake till done. Beat the white of an egg for meringue, spread on top and brown in the oven. Serve with cream or sauce of any kind. —Mrs. Hugh Parry.

GELATINE CUSTARD.

One quart milk, one-half box gelatine, two-thirds cup sugar, three eggs. Put gelatine in milk, scald the same, then add the yolks of eggs with the sugar, and salt. Let it come to a boil; when a little cool stir in the whites. Set it in a basin of cold water and stir thoroughly, adding flavoring when quite cool.

ORANGE JELLY.

One-half box gelatine dissolved in one-half pint cold water half an hour; then add half a pint boiling water, place over the steam of a tea-kettle. When thoroughly dissolved add one cup sugar, the juice of five oranges and two lemons, and put in a mould in a cool place.

PRUNE JELLY.

Soak in water one-half a box of gelatine. Stew half a pound of prunes until tender, then remove the stones. To liquid add gelatine and one cup of sugar, and enough hot water to make a pint and a gill of liquid. Return prunes to liquid and let boil. Serve with whipped cream.

WHIPPED CREAM.

Add to one-half pint cream of moderate thickness the white of one egg beaten to a stiff froth, one-half cup pulverized sugar and flavoring. The grated rind and juice of half a lemon is nice.

CHARLOTTE RUSSE.

Eighteen Savoy biscuit, three-fourths pint cream, one table-spoon powdered sugar, one-half ounce isinglass. Flavor with vanilla or wine. Brush the biscuit with the white of egg. Line the bottom of a round mould, standing them upright all around the edge, then place the mould in the oven for five minutes to dry the egg. Whip the cream to a stiff froth with the sugar, flavoring and melted isinglass. Fill the charlotte, cover the top with a piece of sponge cake the shape of the mould, place on the ice until ready for use.—Mrs. WERNER.

WINE JELLY.

Two pounds sugar, one pint pale sherry, one pint cold water, one package Cox's gelatine, juice of two lemons, one quart boiling water, small stick cinnamon. Soak the gelatine in cold water one hour, add to this sugar, lemon, cinnamon, and pour over all the boiling water, stirring until gelatine is dissolved. Put in the wine last. Strain through flannel bag without squeezing. Wet mould with cold water and pour in the jelly; set on ice to cool.—Mrs. WERNER.

ICE - CREAM.

One teacup milk, one cup sugar, two eggs beaten light, let come to a boil; cool and strain, adding one quart cream. Flavor with a tablespoon of vanilla. Then freeze.—Mrs. McKENZIE.

COFFEE JELLY.

One box gelatine dissolved in half a pint cold water two hours, then add one pint sugar, one pint strong hot coffee, one and a half pints boiling water. Strain and set away to cool. Serve with cream and sugar.—Miss R. H. NASH.

ORANGE SHERBET.

Six oranges, whites of six eggs beaten to a stiff froth, two quarts of water, two cups of sugar. Freeze same as ice cream. —Mrs. Paxton.

LEMON JELLY.

One-half paper gelatine dissolved in one-half pint cold water an hour; then add one pint of boiling water, juice of a lemon, three-fourths pint sugar. Strain and set away to cool.

CHARLOTTE RUSSE.

One pint milk, one-fourth box Nelson's gelatine, two cups sugar, yolks of two eggs. Mix these ingredients and set in a vessel of boiling water until gelatine is dissolved. Strain through a sieve. Flavor with vanilla. When cool, beat in one pint of well-whipped cream. Line your dish with sponge cake and pour in the custard.—Mrs. J. B. Henslee.

FRUIT ICE-CREAM.

Two quarts cream, five eggs, one and one-fourth coffee-cups pulverized sugar, three pounds peaches peeled and chopped fine. Beat whites and yolks of eggs separately. Any fruit preferred may be used.—Mrs. Guilbault.

ICE-CREAM.

One pint of milk, one pint of cream, one cup pulverized sugar, two eggs. Flavor to suit the taste. This makes three pints of cream.—Mrs. G. B. Harker.

PINEAPPLE SHERBET.

Pour two quarts of boiling water over one can of sliced pineapple, steep one hour and strain. Add juice of six lemons and two cups of sugar. Put into freezer; when partly frozen, whip the whites of five eggs to a stiff froth, adding slowly after they are whipped four tablespoons pulverized sugar. Stir this slowly into freezer and freeze two hours.—Mrs. H. C. Dimick.

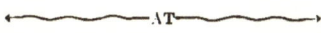

CREAMED OYSTERS.

One quart of oysters, one and a half cups cream, one heaping tablespoon cornstarch. Salt and pepper to taste. Let the cream come to a boil, mix the cornstarch in a little milk and stir into the cream, add pepper and salt. Let the oysters come to a boil in their own liquor, and skim carefully. Drain off the liquor, and turn the oysters into the cream.—MRS. H. D. LEONARD.

CREAMED CELERY.

Cut in inch pieces and cover with milk, to which, when boiling, add salt and a small piece of butter. Serve hot.

DICED TURNIPS.

Pare, slice, cut in dice an inch square; boil until nearly done in as little water as possible. To one quart of turnips, add one tablespoon sugar, and salt to taste; when boiled quite dry, add two or three spoons of cream and a beaten egg.—MRS. A. J. LAMPSHIRE.

CHOPPED PICKLE.

One peck of green tomatoes, one pint green peppers, two quarts green cucumbers, four bunches celery and one ounce celery seed, one ounce mustard seed, five cents worth of tumeric in a bag, one large cup brown sugar, two heads of cabbage, one-fourth pound horse-radish. Sprinkle salt over cabbage and tomatoes, and let drain over night; rinse with water in the morning. Put seeds and tumeric in vinegar and boil, pour over the ingredients while hot.

EGG OMELETTE.

Ten eggs, one large coffee-cup milk, a little salt. Beat the eggs very light, add the milk and salt. Pour into a hot skillet in which a large tablespoon of butter has been melted. When partly cooked, remove from fire and bake in oven until firm. Place a hot platter on top of omelette, invert quickly, and serve at once.

CHILI SAUCE.

Fifty large, ripe tomatoes, six green peppers, six red peppers, eight onions and six garlics, eight tablespoons salt, eight tablespoons sugar, twelve cups vinegar, celery, cloves, cinnamon and allspice to taste. Chop peppers and onions very fine. Peel and chop the tomatoes. Boil two hours; stir while boiling.

WATERMELON SWEET PICKLE.

Pare and cut the rind into thin pieces and place in a porcelain-lined kettle; to about five pounds of fruit, add two teaspoons salt, with sufficient water to cover, and boil until tender enough to pierce with a silver fork. Drain well, then take one quart of vinegar, two pounds sugar, and pour over the fruit. Scald the syrup and pour over the fruit for eight successive days, the ninth day add one ounce each stick cinnamon, whole cloves and allspice. Scald all together and seal up. Nicer if left to stand two or three months.—MRS. L. A. GROVER.

DRESSING FOR MEATS AND POULTRY.

ESPECIALLY FOR TURKEYS.

One-half loaf baker's bread dried and soaked in cold water; squeeze the bread well with the hands until all the water is out. Smother a *small* onion in a large piece of butter, but do not brown it; add this to the bread, also one pound chopped veal, one-half pound tender pork, grated half nutmeg, pepper, salt, chopped parsley, three eggs, beating the whites to a froth and adding last.—MRS. WERNER.

VEAL LOAF.

Three-fourths pound raw veal, one-fourth pound raw salt-pork, three eggs, nine crackers, three teaspoons salt, one and a half teaspoons pepper, parsley. Chop very fine, and bake one hour. When cold, slice thin.—Mrs. W. H. Nash.

GERMAN PICKLES.

One bushel large, yellow cucumbers; peel, cut up lengthwise and remove seeds; sprinkle with salt and let stand twelve hours. Strain and thoroughly dry with a cloth; cover with cold vinegar and let stand for two weeks; pour off vinegar, dry cucumbers, put in a jar with a teacup of mustard seeds and spices. Boil sufficient vinegar to cover and pour over them warm.—Mrs. Werner.

ESCALLOPED OYSTERS.

Sprinkle a buttered dish with cracker crumbs, then put in a layer of oysters, some bits of butter, a little pepper and salt, and so on until the dish is full, leaving crumbs and butter on top. Pour over the top a little milk. Bake until of a light brown.

TO BLANCH ALMONDS.

Shell the nuts and pour boiling water over them; let them stand a minute, then throw them into cold water; rub between the hands and the dark skin will come off.

BOILED FISH.

One mountain trout or white fish, clean and wash well, sprinkle salt on the inside and out and let it stand over night; in the morning put into salt boiling water, boiling fifteen or twenty minutes. Lay on a platter sprinkled with chopped parsley and serve at once with hot potatoes boiled in salt water. For gravy, a large piece of butter melted but not boiled; pour the butter slowly into a tureen, leaving the salt in the dish. Add chopped parsley.—Mrs. Werner.

SPICED CURRANTS.

Stem three pints of ripe currants. Make a syrup of three parts of sugar to one of strong vinegar. Add currants, boil for a few minutes, stirring constantly to prevent burning. Spice with cinnamon and cloves.—Mrs. H. C. Dimick.

FISH CHOWDER.

Try out small pieces of salt pork in a kettle. Cut up a medium-sized fish, slice thin four or five potatoes ; add these to the salt pork in alternate layers; cover with boiling water and cook until soft. Season to taste, add an onion if liked, one large pint milk, and piece of butter. Let boil. Add a few Boston crackers (split) just before serving.

GRAPE PRESERVES.

Wash the grapes, weigh, having equal weight of sugar and grapes ; then pulp the grapes, put the pulp in a kettle and boil twenty-five minutes. Rub through a sieve ; return this to the kettle, add the sugar, and boil thirty minutes, then put in the skins and boil ten minutes.—Miss R. H. Nash.

DUMPLINGS.

One pint flour, one cup milk, one egg, a large teaspoon baking powder, little salt. Make the batter soft, so as to drop in with a spoon. Cook about ten minutes. Be sure to have the soup boiling when you drop them in. Serve at once.—Mrs. W. H. Nash.

SAUER KRAUT WITH OYSTERS.

Drain the oysters. Mix some flour with part of the liquor, put the rest of the liquor on the stove, let come to a boil; add oysters and flour and let come to a boil again ; add pepper and salt and piece of butter. Then fill dish with layer of sauer kraut and layer of oysters alternately. Serve at once.—Mrs. Werner.

SWEET PICKLE.

Take seven pounds of fruit, three pounds sugar, one quart vinegar, one-half ounce each mace, cinnamon and cloves, and scald all together. Take out the fruit and boil the syrup down and pour over; repeat this for three days.

COLD TOMATO CATSUP.

One-half peck tomatoes, three pints of good vinegar, three-fourths cup salt, three-fourths cup ground mustard seed, three peppers, handful celery seed, one tablespoon grated horse-radish. Mix well and bottle tight.

SPICED BEEF.

Chop one pound raw beefsteak and a piece of suet or pork the size of an egg. Add one-half pint bread crumbs or crackers, two eggs, six tablespoons cream or milk, a small piece of butter. Season with savory, marjoram, salt and pepper. Mix and make in a roll with flour enough to keep together. Bake. When cold slice thin.

PREPARED FISH.

Boil until quite soft three pounds of fish; pick in small pieces and lay upon a flat dish. Season with pepper and salt, add a small piece of butter. Turn upon the well-beaten yolks of four eggs a pint of scalding milk, and pour it over the fish. Beat to a stiff froth the whites and spread over the surface. Bake half an hour.—Mrs. W. H. Nash.

TOMATO TOAST.

Run a quart of stewed ripe tomatoes through a colander, place in a porcelain kettle, season with butter, pepper, salt and sugar to taste. Cut thin slices of bread, brown on both sides, place on a platter, and when ready to serve, add a pint of sweet cream to the tomatoes and pour over the toast.—Mrs. A. J. Lampshire.

CRANBERRY JELLY.

Cover cranberries with water and cook until soft; mash through a colander. To one pint of juice add one pound of sugar. Return to stove and boil one-half hour. Pour the hot liquid in moulds to cool.—Miss R. H. Nash.

HOT MUSH BREAD FOR DINNER.

Scald a pint of corn meal until of the consistency of mush; when cooked, cool with sour or buttermilk until about as thick as batter cake dough; then add one-half teaspoon each of salt and soda, two eggs, and a teaspoon of butter. Beat well and bake quickly. To be served in the dish in which it is baked, and helped with a spoon.—Mrs. Cooper.

FOAM SAUCE.

One cup sugar, one egg; beat well together, add four table-spoons boiling milk. Flavor with vanilla.—Mrs. W. H. Nash.

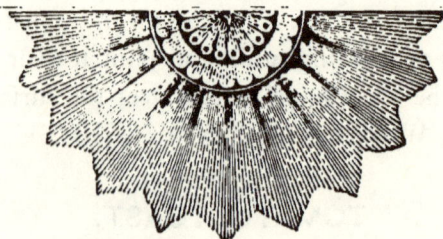

Candies.

MOLASSES CANDY.

Two cups New Orleans molasses, one cup sugar, one table-spoon vinegar, a piece of butter the size of a walnut. Boil twenty-five minutes, stirring constantly. Either pull it or pour out thin on pans.—MISS F. L. RAYMOND.

PEANUT CANDY.

One pound of granulated sugar put in an iron spider; stir until free from lumps. Crush a quart of peanuts very fine and add just before taking from the stove.—MRS. C. E. DODGE.

CHOCOLATE CARAMELS.

One large cup sugar, one-half cup molasses, one half cup milk, butter the size of an egg, one teaspoon cornstarch, one-fourth pound chocolate.—MISS R. H. NASH.

CHOCOLATE CARAMELS.

One cup milk, two cups molasses, one cup sugar, one and a half cakes chocolate, small piece of butter. Grate the chocolate and stir it into the milk when boiling, then stir in gradually the other ingredients. Try it as you would molasses candy, and when done and cooled a little, cut in squares half an inch.

FRENCH CREAM CANDY.

(UNCOOKED.)

Mix whites of two eggs and their bulk in water in a large bowl; beat very well, add a dessert spoon vanilla and about two pounds "XXX" confectioners' sugar (finest grade of powdered sugar), well sifted; beat well, and the paste is ready. Take half a pound of dates, remove stones, put in a piece of the candy paste and roll each one in granulated sugar.

For Fig Candy, split half a pound of figs, place a layer of the dough on a board (first sprinkle well with powdered sugar to prevent its adhering), then a layer of figs, again a layer of dough, and cut in squares.

Nuts of any kind may be made up into candy by using the meats for the foundation or inside of little balls of paste, and then roll in coarse sugar; set each kind out in a cool place to harden.

For Chocolate Creams roll any number of balls size of small marbles from the dough, and when they are hardened, dip with a fork into some Baker's chocolate melted on the stove. Be careful not to allow it to boil; better to melt it in a little cup placed in a pan of hot water on the stove. Or make a caramel of three-fourths pint sugar, one-third pint milk, two tablespoons butter, and one square chocolate. Boil twenty minutes and add one teaspoon vanilla. Remove from fire, place in a pan of hot water, and dip in the little balls.

Cocoanut Candy may be made by rolling out another portion of the dough on the floured board, sprinkle with cocoanut, roll a few times with the roller, and cut into squares.

A mixture of cocoanut and nuts chopped fine makes a delicious candy.

For English Walnut Candy split the walnuts, shape some of the dough into round flat balls, place a half of the nut on each and press firmly. Use hickory-nut meats for Hickory-Nut Candy.

∴ To clean the silver spoons and forks in everyday use, rub them with a damp cloth dipped in baking soda, then polish them with a small piece of chamois skin.

* *
*

∴ Rub salt on the inside of your coffee pot when washing it, and it will remove the coffee and egg very quickly. Be sure to rinse it thoroughly before using it again.

* *
*

∴ Old lamp burners should be boiled often in strong saleratus water. Let them boil for an hour, polish them, and they will be as good as new, and will not trouble you by causing a smoky light. * *
*

∴ Brooms become very brittle in this dry atmosphere; dipping them in hot suds every week will toughen them, so they will last much longer. * *
*

∴ Cut old boot tops into pieces the right size, cover with calico, and you have a holder that will not heat the hand.

JAVELLE WATER.

TO BLEACH AND REMOVE STAINS.

Four pounds sal-soda, one pound chloride of lime, one gallon water. Heat the sal soda in a vessel over the fire, add the water boiling. Boil ten minutes. Add the chloride of lime, having first reduced it to powder. When cold, bottle and cork the mixture. Rinse well after using.

CLEANING FLUID.

Sulphuric ether, one drachm; chloroform, one drachm; alcohol, two drachms; deodorized benzine, two pints; oil of wintergreen, two drachms. Nice for cleaning kid gloves, grease spots, etc.